United States, David Hunter

Report of the Military Services of Gen. David Hunter, U.S.A.

during the war of the rebellion, made to the U.S. War department, 1873.

Second Edition

United States, David Hunter

Report of the Military Services of Gen. David Hunter, U.S.A.
during the war of the rebellion, made to the U.S. War department, 1873. Second Edition

ISBN/EAN: 9783337120108

Printed in Europe, USA, Canada, Australia, Japan

Cover: Foto ©ninafisch / pixelio.de

More available books at **www.hansebooks.com**

REPORT

OF

THE MILITARY SERVICES

OF

GEN. DAVID HUNTER, U.S.A.,

DURING

The War of the Rebellion,

MADE TO THE

U. S. WAR DEPARTMENT,

1873.

———

SECOND EDITION.

———

NEW YORK:

D. VAN NOSTRAND COMPANY, Publishers,

Nos. 23 MURRAY AND 27 WARREN STREET,

———

[1873.]
1892.

Private

Executive Mansion
Washington D.C. April 1. 1863.

Major General Hunter.
My dear Sir:

I am glad to see the accounts of your colored force at Jacksonville, Florida. I see the enemy are driving at them fiercely, as is to be expected. It is important to them, nay, that such a force shall _not_ take shape, and grow, and thrive, in the South; and in precisely the same proportion, it is important to us that it _shall._ Hence the utmost caution and vigilance is necessary on our part. The enemy will make extra efforts to destroy them; and we should do the same to preserve and increase them.

Yours truly,
A. Lincoln

EDITOR'S PREFACE.

This brochure is an advanced chapter of the "Memoirs of General David Hunter." It is published in view of the encampment of the G. A. R. in this city, on the 20th of September. It is feared by some good friends that it may prejudice the sale and circulation of the complete work. "Per contra"—others think it will rather promote than repress those aims. To these advisors I have deferred.

MOSES HOGE HUNTER.

Washington, D. C.

REPORT.

War Department, Adjutant-General's Office,
Washington, April 25, 1873.

Colonel David Hunter, *U. S. Army*, 1726
I Street, Washington, D. C.:

Sir: In response to your verbal request
of yesterday, I have the honor to furnish the
following extract from the communication from
this Office, dated June 14, 1872, calling for a
report of your military services during the
war:

"With a view to uniformity in the reports,
please state date of assuming and being relieved from each command; how subsequently
employed; date and period of each leave of
absence: if on court-martial or military commission, when, where, and for what period;
name of President and Judge-Advocate; also.
name, rank, and period of service of each of

your staff-officers, with a brief summary of each battle in which you were engaged, and report on letter paper, leaving one inch margin on left-hand side for binding."

In regard to the extent or minuteness of the report, you are at liberty to exercise your own pleasure, and also consult your own time and convenience in its preparation.

While an outline sketch might answer all practical purposes, yet a detailed narrative is preferred.

Very respectfully, your obedient servant,

J. P. MARTIN,

Assist. Adjutant-General.

In compliance with the above order, I have the honor to report that I was born in the State of New Jersey, graduated from the Military Academy at West Point, in 1822, served eleven years in the infantry, and was then selected for promotion, as Captain, in the new regiment of dragoons, in which I served for three years. Having, for reasons connected with my private affairs, withdrawn from the army for a few years, I renewed my connection with it in 1841, in the Pay Department, serving with the Army under Gen. TAYLOR, through the late war with Mexico. During the Presidential campaign which issued in the election of Mr. LINCOLN, I was stationed at Fort Leavenworth, Kansas. Many of the officers of the garrison were of Southern origin and sympathies, and they freely discussed the political questions then agitating the country. By one of their number it was distinctly stated that the South would not allow the inauguration of an "abolition President"; that if Mr. LINCOLN were elected, he would not be permitted to go to Washington; that four years previously, arrangements had been made to prevent the inauguration of Gen. FREMONT in case of his election; that the Governors of Virginia and Maryland were each to furnish ten thousand men, and the other States of the South their quota; that they were to take possession of Washington, and make Mr. PIERCE hold over until they had perfected their arrangement. Believing then, as I do now, the substantial truth of these representations, and feeling assured of Mr. LINCOLN's election, I deemed it my duty to communicate this information to him, and to urge upon him to induce his friends to take efficient means to secure his peaceable inauguration, and to render certain the possession of the seat of Government. I have several notes from Mr. LINCOLN on this subject.

SERVICES IN WASHINGTON.

After the election, I was invited by Mr LINCOLN to accompany him to Washington; and his inauguration having been accomplished, I was ordered by Gen. SCOTT to take charge of the Presidential mansion. For six weeks I spent every night in the East Room, where I could receive the reports of my guard without disturbing the members of the family. This guard consisted of about one hundred gentlemen from all parts of the Union, who, on being apprised of the danger, cheerfully enrolled themselves for service.

On the 14th of May, 1861, I was appointed Colonel of the Sixth Cavalry, a new regiment just then added to the regular army. As the volunteers arrived in Washington, I was ordered to the command of a brigade, called the Brigade of the Aqueduct, stationed on the Virginia hill, immediately opposite Georgetown.

FIRST BATTLE OF BULL RUN.

I was relieved from the command of the Brigade of the Aqueduct by Gen. W. T. SHERMAN, then Colonel of the Thirteenth Infantry, in June, 1861, and ordered to take command of the Right Division of the army about to advance on the enemy, in the vicinity of Manassas. That division I commanded at the battle of Bull Run, July 21, 1861. I was wounded in the neck shortly after the commencement of the battle, while endeavoring to induce my advanced guard to charge the enemy with the bayonet. Gen. ANDREW PORTER, who commanded my first brigade, assumed command on being informed that I was disabled. The loss of that battle an all-wise Providence overruled to a great success.

After the battle of Bull Run I was appointed a Brigadier-General of Volunteers, to date from May 17, 1861 ; and a Major-General of Volunteers, to date from August 13, 1861.

CAMPAIGN IN MISSOURI.

When sufficiently recovered from my wound
to admit of active du:y, I was ordered to
report to Gen. FREMONT, then in command
of the Western Department, with his headquarters at St. Louis. I commanded the First
Division of Gen. FREMONT'S army in its advance on Springfield, Missouri; and on the
2d of November, 1861, I relieved Gen. FRE-
MONT in command of the Western Department, at Springfield, by order of the President,
at the same time receiving from the President
the following autographic letter:

WASHINGTON, Oct. 24, 1861.

SIR: The command of the Department of
the West having devolved upon you, I propose
to offer you a few *suggestions*, knowing how haz-
ardous it is to bind down a distant commander
in the field to specific lines and operations, as
so much always depends on a knowledge of
localities and passing events. It is intended,
therefore, to leave a considerable margin for
the exercise of your judgment and discretion.

The main rebel army (PRICE'S) west of the
Mississippi is believed to have passed Dale

County, in full retreat upon Northwestern
Arkansas, leaving Missouri almost freed from
the enemy, excepting in the southeast of the
State. Assuming this basis of facts, it seems de-
sirable, as you are not likely to overtake PRICE,
and are in danger of making too long a line
from your own base of supplies and reinforcements, that you should give up the pursuit,
halt your main army, divide it into two corps
of observation, one occupying Sedalia, and the
other Rolla, the present *termini* of railroads;
then recruit the condition of both corps, by
re-establishing and inproving their discipline
and instruction; perfecting their clothing and
equipments, and providing less uncomfortable
quarters. Of course, both railroads must be
guarded and kept open, judiciously employing
just as much force as is necessary for this.
From these two points, Sedalia and Rolla, and
especially in judicious co-operation with LANE
on the Kansas border, it would be so easy to
concentrate, and repel any army of the enemy
returing on Missouri from the Southwest,
that it is not probable any such attempt to
return will be made before or during the

approaching cold weather.

Before spring, the people of Missouri will be in no favorable mood to renew, for the next year, the troubles which have so much afflicted and impoverished them during this.

If you adopt this line of policy, and if, as I anticipate, you will see no enemy in great force approaching, you will have a surplus of force, which you can withdraw from these points and direct to others, as may be needed, the railroads furnishing ready means for reinforcing these main points if occasion requires.

Doubtless local uprisings, for a time, will continue to occur; but these can be met by detachments and local forces of our own, and will, ere long, tire out of themselves.

While, as stated in the beginning of this letter, a large discretion must be, and is, left to yourself, I feel sure that an indefinite pursuit of PRICE, or an attempt by this long and circuitous route to reach Memphis, will be exhaustive beyond endurance, and will end in the loss of the whole force engaged in it.

Your obedient servant,

A. LINCOLN.

To the Commander of the
Department of the West.

I give this letter of Mr. Lincoln in full to show the soundness of his judgment even in military affairs. The idea of chasing Price into the wilds of Western Arkansas, and thus putting the army entirely out of position, and preventing operations on the lower Mississippi during the winter, was so absurd that I should not have thought of it for a moment, even if I had not had the good advice of Mr. Lincoln.

I arrived at Springfield, on the night of the 1st of November, with orders in my possession to relieve Gen. Fremont. I immediately went to the General's quarters, and found him in the midst of a Council of War, planning an attack on the enemy at daylight the next morning, at Wilson's Creek. As soon as an opportunity offered, one of his Generals whispered to me not to concern myself about the Council or the attack at daylight, as there was no enemy within sixty miles of Wilson's Creek. This statement I found to be literally true.

SERVICES IN KANSAS.

On the 9th of November, 1861, I was relieved of the command of the Western Department, by the order of Gen. GEO. B. McCLELLAN, and ordered to the command of the Department of Kansas. Under date of Dec. 11, 1861, Gen. McCLELLAN writes to me : In regard to placing Gen. HALLECK in command of the Department of Missouri, that step was taken from the evident necessity of placing some one there who was in no manner connected, *for or against*, with the unfortunate state of affairs previously existing in that Department." The meaning of that sentence I was not able to determine.

During my short stay in Kansas, it was my good fortune to render important service, not in the field; for there was not an enemy within my Department, but by furnishing, from my own small force, assistance to neighboring commanders. At this time I was superior in rank to Gen. HALLECK and also to Gen. CANBY, then commanding in New Mexico. They both appealed to me for assistance, and on my own responsibility I sent them help. In a

telegram, Gen. HALLECK thus frankly acknow-
ledges my assistance :

ST. LOUIS, Feb. 19, 1862.

MAJOR-GENERAL HUNTER, *Department of Kansas :*

To you, more than any other man in this
Department, are we indebted for our success
at Fort Donelson. In my strait for troops to
reinforce Gen. GRANT, I appealed to you.
You nobly and generously placed your forces
at my disposition. This enabled us to win the
victory. Receive my most heartfelt thanks.

H. W. HALLECK,

Major-General.

At the same time, I took the responsibility
of sending Gen. JOHN P. SLOUGH'S regiment
of mounted Colorado Volunteers, by forced
marches, to Gen. CANBY'S assistance in New
Mexico. This regiment gained a splendid
victory over the enemy at the Canon Glori-
etta, which, it is acknowledged, saved New
Mexico.

DEPARTMENT OF THE SOUTH.

Having been ordered to the Department of the South, I assumed command of that department March 31, 1862, relieving Gen. THOMAS W. SHERMAN. I commanded at the bombardment of Fort Pulaski, Georgia, on the 10th and 11th of April, 1862. As this fort had been pronounced impregnable by the chief engineers of both services, we were quite surprised to see their flag come down after a bombardment of only thirty hours. The expensive mortar batteries, chiefly relied on for the reduction of this fort, were utterly worthless, not one of the large shells having been thrown into the fort.

The constant and urgent demands for men in every direction rendered it impossible for the War Department to send me the promised reinforcements.

I left the Department of the South on the 3d of Sept., 1862, on leave of absence, and came to Washington, hoping to obtain more active employment. On the 23d of the same month, I was detailed as president of a court-martial for the trial of Gen. Fitzjohn Porter: Gen. Holt, Judge-Advocate General, assisted by the Hon. John A. Bingham, of Ohio, being the Judge-Advocate. On the 21st of January, 1863, I was relieved from that duty, and ordered back to the Department of the South.

ARMING THE NEGROES.

While in this command I issued an order freeing the slaves in South Carolina, Georgia and Florida, the States composing my Department—my theory being that slavery, existing only by municipal enactments, ceased to exist the moment a subject by his rebellion placed himself beyond the pale of these enactments. I also enlisted a regiment of these freedmen. Mr. Lincoln repudiated, *in the newspapers*, my order freeing the slaves, but he never sent me his proclamation or the first word of disapprobation; on the contrary, I believe he rejoiced in my action, and his great interest in the colored troops is shown by the following characteristic letter:

[Private.]

"Executive Mansion, Washington,
"April 1, 1863.

"Major-General Hunter:

"My Dear Sir: I am glad to see the accounts of your colored force at Jacksonville, Florida. I see the enemy are driving at them fiercely, as is to be expected. It is important to the enemy that such force shall *not* take shape and grow and thrive in the South; and in precisely the same proportion it is important to us that it *shall*. Hence the utmost caution and vigilance are necessary on our part. The enemy will make extra efforts to destroy them, and we should do the same to preserve and increase them.

"Yours truly,

"A. LINCOLN."

From the beginning I urged upon the Government, in the strongest terms, the enlistment of negro troops, the former slaves of the rebels, not only as adding to the number and efficiency of our own forces, but chiefly on account of its depriving the enemy of just so much labor in their fields, and compelling them to send an equal number of white men to do the necessary cultivation. The regiment of negroes which I enlisted in South Carolina on my own responsibility was a great success. The men aquired the drill with great rapidity; they were subordinate and attentive to all their duties, and particularly successful on picket duty. I made repeated efforts in vain to get this regiment recognized and paid by the Government. It was a delicate subject, and I could get no reply approving or disapproving my conduct in this matter. Fortunately for me, however, the Hon. Mr. WICKLIFFE, of Kentucky, conceiving I had committed a heinous crime, introduced a denunciatory resolution in the House of Representatives. This resolution was referred to me by the Hon. Secretary of War, and my report in reply was immediately sent to Congress. That report is as follows:

" HEADQUARTERS, DEPARTMENT OF THE SOUTH,
" HILTON HEAD, S. C., June, 1862.

"TO THE HON. E. M. STANTON, *Secretary of War, Washington, D. C.:*

" SIR : I have the honor to acknowledge the receipt of a communication from the Adjutant-General of the Army, dated June 13, 1862, requesting me to furnish you with the information necessary to answer certain resolutions introduced in the House of Representatives, June 9, 1862, on motion of the Hon. Mr. WICKLIFFE, of Kentucky, their substance being to enquire :

" 1. Whether I had organized, or was organizing, a regiment of 'fugitive slaves' in this Department?

" 2. Whether any authority had been given to me from the War Department for such organization ; and,

" 3. Whether I had been furnished, by order of the War Department, with clothing, uniforms, arms, equipments, and so forth, for such a force ?

"Only having received the letter at a late

hour this evening, I urge forward my answer in time for the steamer sailing to-morrow morning—this haste preventing me from entering as minutely as I could wish upon many points of detail, such as the paramount importance of the subject would seem to call for. But, in view of the near termination of the present session of Congress, and the widespread interest which must have been awakened by Mr. WICKLIFFE's resolutions, I prefer sending even this imperfect answer to waiting the period necessary for the collection of fuller and more comprehensive data.

"To the first question, therefore, I reply: that no regiment of ' fugitive slaves ' has been or is being organized in this department. There is, however, a fine regiment of loyal persons whose late masters are ' fugitive rebels '—men who everywhere fly before the appearance of the national flag, leaving their loyal and unhappy servants behind them to shift, as best they can, for themselves. So far, indeed, are the loyal persons composing this regiment from seeking to evade the presence of their late owners, that they are now, one and all, endeavoring with commendable zeal to acquire the drill and discipline requisite to place them in a position to go in full and effective pursuit of their fugacious and traitorous proprietors.

"To the second question, I have the honor to answer that the instructions given to Brig.-Gen. T. W. SHERMAN by the Hon. SIMON CAMERON, late Secretary of War, and turned over to me, by succession, for my guidance, do distinctly authorize me to employ 'all loyal persons offering their services in defence of the Union, and for the suppression of this rebellion,' in any manner I may see fit, or that circumstances may call for. There is no restriction as to the character or color of the persons to be employed, or the nature of the employments—whether civil or military—in which their services may be used. I conclude, therefore, that I have been authorized to enlist 'fugitive slaves' as soldiers, could any such fugitives be found in this Department.

"No such characters, however, have yet appeared within view of our most advanced pickets—the loyal negroes everywhere remaining on their plantations to welcome us, aid us, and supply us with food, labor, and information. It is the masters who have in every instance been the 'fugitives,' running away from loyal slaves as well as loyal soldiers; and these, as yet, we have only partially been able to see—chiefly their heads over ramparts, or dodging behind trees, rifle in hand, in the extreme distance. In the absence of any 'Fugitive Master Law,' the deserted slaves would be wholly without remedy, had not the crime of treason given the right to pursue, capture, and bring back those persons of whose benignant protection they have been thus suddenly and cruelly bereft.

"To the third interrogatory, it is my painful duty to reply that I have never received any specific authority for issues of clothing, uniforms, arms, equipments, and so forth, to the troops in question—my general instructions from Mr. CAMERON, to employ them in any manner I might find necessary, and the military exigencies of the Department and the country, being my only, but I trust sufficient,

justification. Neither have I had any specific
authority for supplying these persons with
shovels, spades, and pickaxes, when employing them as laborers; nor with boats and oars
when using them as lightermen; but these
are not points included in Mr. WICKLIFFE'S
resolution. To me it seemed that liberty to
employ men in any particular capacity im-
plied and carried with it liberty, also, to
supply them with the necessary tools;
and, acting upon this faith, I have clothed,
equipped, and armed the only loyal regiment
yet raised in South Carolina, Georgia, or
Florida.

"I must say, in vindication of my own conduct, that had it not been for the many other
diversified and imperative claims upon my
time and attention, a much more satisfactory
result might have been achieved; and that in
place of only one regiment, as at present, at
least five or six well-drilled, brave, and thoroughly acclimated regiments should by this
time have been added to the loyal forces of
the Union.

" The experiment of arming the blacks, so far as I have made it, has been a complete and marvellous success. They are sober, docile, attentive, and enthusiastic—displaying great natural capacities in acquiring the duties of the soldier. They are now eager beyond all things to take the field and be led into action ; and it is the unanimous opinion of the officers who have had charge of them, that, in the peculiarities of this climate and country, they will prove invaluable auxiliaries—fully equal to the similar regiments so long and successfully used by the British authorities in the West India Islands.

" In conclusion, I would say, it is my hope, there appearing no possibility of other reinforcements—owning to the exigencies of the campaign in the Peninsula—to have organized by the end of next fall, and be able to present to the Government, from forty-eight to fifty thousand of these hardy and devoted soldiers.

"Trusting that this letter may be made part of your answer to Mr. WICKLIFFE'S reso-

lutions, I have the honor to be, very respectfully,

"Your most obedient servant,

(Signed) DAVID HUNTER,

"*Major-General Commanding.*"

"This missive was duly sent, with many
misgivings that it would not get through the
routine of the War Department in time to be
laid before Congress previous to the adjourn-
ment of that honorable body, which was then
imminent. There were fears, too, that the
Secretary of War might think it not sufficiently
respectful, or serious in its tone ; but such ap-
prehensions proved unfounded. The moment
it was received and read in the War Department, it was hurried down to the House, and
delivered, *ore rotundo.* from the Clerk's desk.
Here its effect, was magical. The clerk could
scarcely read it with decorum ; nor could half
his words be heard amidst the universal peals
of laughter in which both Democrats and Re-
publicans appeared to vie as to which should
be the more noisy. Mr. WICKLIFFE, who only
entered during the reading of the latter half of

the document, rose to his feet in a frenzy of indignation, complaining that the reply, of which he had only heard some portion, was an insult to the dignity of the House, and should be severely noticed.

The more he raved and gesticulated, the more irrepressibly did his colleagues, on both sides of the slavery question, scream and laugh ; until, finally, the merriment reached its climax on a motion of some member—SCHUYLER COLFAX, if we remember rightly—that "as the document appeared to please the honorable gentleman from Kentucky so much, and as he had not heard the whole of it, the clerk be now requested to read the whole again "—a motion which was instantaneously carried amid such an uproar of universal merriment and applause as the frescoed walls of the chamber have seldom heard, either before or since. It was the great joke of the day, and coming at a moment of universal gloom in the public mind, was seized upon by the whole loyal press of the country, as a kind of politico—military champagne cocktail.

This set that question at rest forever ; and not long after, the proper authorities saw fit to authorize the employment of "fifty thousand able-bodied blacks for labor in the Quartermaster's Department," and the arming and drilling as soldiers of five thousand of those—but for the sole purpose of "protecting the women and children of their fellow-laborers who might be absent from home in the public service."

Here we have another instance of the reluctance with which the National Government took up this idea of employing negroes as soldiers—a resoultion, we may add, to which they were only finally compelled by General HUNTER's disbandment of his original regiment, and the storm of public indignation which followed that act."

" Baked Meats of the funeral " pp. 187-9 by Private MILES O'REILLY.

From the same book, I transcribe the 207th page.

"In regard to HUNTER's reply to Mr. WICKLIFFE, we shall only add this anecdote, told us one day by that brilliant gentleman and scholar, the Hon. Sun-set COX, of Ohio :

" I tell you that letter from HUNTER spoiled

the prettiest speech I had ever thought of mak

ing. I had been delighted with WICKLIFFE'S
motion, and thought the reply to it would furnish us first-rate Democratic thunder for the
next election. I made up my mind to sail in
against HUNTER'S answer—no matter what it
was—the moment it came ; and to be even
more humorously successful in its delivery and
reception than I was in my speech against
War- Horse GURLEY, of Ohio, which you have
just been complimenting. Well, you see—
man proposes, but Providence orders otherwise.
When the clerk announced the receipt of the
answer, and that he was about to read it, I
caught the Speaker's eye and was booked for
the first speech against your negro experiment.
The first sentence, being formal and official,
was very well ; but at the second the House
began to grin ; and at the third, not a man on
the floor—except Father WICKLIFFE, of Kentucky, perhaps—who was not convulsed with
laughter. Even my own risibles, I found to be
affected ; and before the document was con-
cluded I motioned the Speaker that he might
give the floor to whom he pleased, as my de-

sire to distinguish myself in that particular tilt was over."

This brought the whole subject before the country, and Congress at once authorized the enlisting of fifty thousand negroes, and subsequently of a still larger number. My poor South Carolina regiment, however, was discharged without pay—martyrs in a good cause. How my action in reference to the enlistment of Southern negroes was regarded by the enemy, is sufficiently evident from the following General Order, issued by the Confederate Government at Richmond :

WAR DEPARTMENT,

ADJUTANT AND INS.-GEN.'S OFFICE,

RICHMOND, August 21, 1862.

General Orders—No. 60.

Whereas, Major-General HUNTER, recently in command of the enemy's forces on the coast of South Carolina, and Brigadier-General PHELPS, a military commander of the enemy in the State of Louisiana, have organized and armed negro slaves for military service against their masters, citizens of this

Confederacy : And whereas, the Government of the United States has refused to answer an enquiry whether said conduct of its officers meets its sanction, and has thus left this Government no other means of repressing said crimes and outrages than the adoption of such measures of retaliation as shall serve to prevent their repetition:

Ordered, that Major-General HUNTER and Brigadier-General PHELPS be no longer held and treated as public enemies of the Confederate States, but as outlaws ; and in the event of the capture of either of them, or that of any other officer employed in drilling, organizing, or instructing slaves, with a view to their armed service in this war, he shall not be regarded as a prisoner of war, but held in close confinement for execution as a felon, at such time and place as the President shall order.

By order,   S. COOPER,
Adjutant and Inspector-General.

This infamous edict was never noticed by our Government, and they went on exchanging prisoners as if no such insult had been offered. I remained under this ban till the end of the war. I, however, took effectual measures to protect my own officers. One of them had been taken prisoner near St. Augustine, Florida, and thrown into the common jail in Charleston. He informed me, by an open letter, sent by a rebel flag of truce, that he was to be sent back to Florida, to be tried by the civil courts on a charge of exciting an insurrection of the negroes. I immediately notified the rebel authorities that I would at once seize and place in close confinement all citizens of any influence within my lines, and would immediately execute three of their number for every one of my officers injured. In a few days, I received another open letter from this officer, saying that he had been released from confinement, was treated most kindly by the people of Charleston, and was, on the first opportunity, to be sent North for exchange.

While in command of the Department of the South, I was off the harbor of Charleston, in the steamer *Ben de Ford*, and witnessed the naval attack on Fort Sumter by nine iron-clads, under the command of Admiral Du Pont. In relation to the situation of affairs in the Department, after this attack, I beg leave to refer to my letter to the President of May 22, 1863, as follows:

"HEADQUARTERS, DEPARTMENT OF THE SOUTH,
"HILTON HEAD, PORT ROYAL, S. C.,
May 22, 1863.

DEAR SIR: It is more than six weeks since the attack by the iron-clads upon Charleston—an attack in which, from the nature of the plans of Admiral DU PONT, the army had no active part.

On the day of that attack, the troops under my command held Folly Island up to Light House Inlet. On the morning after the attack, we were in complete readiness to cross Light House Inlet to Morris Island, where, once established, the fall of Sumter would have been as certain as the demonstration of a problem in mathematics. Aided by a cross-fire from the navy, the enemy would soon have been driven from Cummings' Point; and with powerful batteries of one and two hundred-pounder rifled guns placed there, Fort Sumter would have been rendered untenable in two days' fire. Fort Pulaski was breached and taken from Goat's Point, on Tybee Island, a precisely similar proposition, with 32-pounder Parrot guns, 42-pounder James guns, and a few 10-inch Columbiads; the 13-inch mortars used in that bombardment having proved utterly valueless. I mention these things to show how certain would have been the fall of Fort Sumter under the fire of the one and two hundred pounders, rifled, now at my command.

On the afternoon of the iron-clad attack on Fort Sumter, the troops on Folly Island were not only ready to cross Light House Inlet, but were almost in the act, the final reconnoissance having been made, the boats ready, and the men under arms for crossing, when they were recalled, as I hoped merely temporarily, by the announcement of Admiral Du Pont that he had resolved to retire, and that consquently we could expect no assistance from the navy.

Immediately the Admiral was waited upon

by an officer of my staff, who represented the
forwardness of our preparations for crossing,
the evidently unprepared condition of the
enemy to receive us; while any delay, now
that our intentions were unmasked, would give
the enemy time to erect upon the southern
end of Morris Island, commanding Light
House Inlet, those works and batteries which
he had heretofore neglected. To these con-
siderations, earnestly and elaborately urged,
the Admiral's answer was that he "would not
fire another shot."

A lodgment on Morris Island was thus
made impossible for us, the enemy having
powerful works on the island, more especially
at the northern end, out of which we could
not hope to drive him unless aided by a cross-
fire from the navy. I therefore determined
to hold what we had got until the Admiral
should have had time to repair his vessels;
and to this hour we hold every inch of ground
on Folly and Cole's and Seabrook's Islands that
we held on the day of the expected crossing.

Since then I have exercised patience with
the Admiral, and have pushed forward my

works and batteries on Folly Island with unre-
mitting diligence : the enemy, meanwhile, tho--
roughly aroused to their danger, throwing up
works that completely commanded Light House
Inlet, on the southern end of Morris Island; so
that the crossing which could have been effect-
ed in a couple of hours, and with little sacrifice,
six weeks ago, will now involve, whenever
attempted, protracted operations and a very
serious loss of life. And to what end should
this sacrifice be made without the co-operation
of the navy? Even when established on the
southern end of Morris Island, the northern
end, with its powerful works, and commanded
by the fire of Forts Sumter and Johnson,
would still remain to be possessed. The
sacrifice would be of no avail without the aid
of the navy; and I have been painfully but
finally convinced that from the navy no such
aid is to be expected. I fear Admiral Du
Pont distrusts the iron-clads so much that he
has resolved to do nothing with them this
summer; and, therefore, I most urgently beg
of you to liberate me from those orders to
"co-operate with the navy" which now tie me

down to share the Admiral's inactivity. Remaining in our present situation, we do not even detain one soldier of the enemy from service elsewhere. I am well satisfied that they have already sent away from Charleston and Savannah all the troops not absolutely needed to garrison the defences, and these will have to remain in the works whether an enemy be in sight or not.

Liberate me from this order to "co-operate with the navy in an attack on Charleston," and I will immediately place a column of ten thousand of the best-drilled soldiers in the country (as unquestionably are the troops of this Department) in the heart of Georgia, our landing and marching being made through counties in which, as shown by the census, the slave population is 75 per cent. of the inhabitants. Nothing is truer, sir, than that this rebellion has left the Southern States a mere hollow shell. If we avoid their few strongholds, where they have prepared for and invited us to battle, we shall meet no opposition in a total devastation of their resources ; thus compelling them to

break up their large armies and garrisons
at a few points into scores of small fractions
of armies for the protection of every threatened
or assailable point. I will guarantee, with the
troops now fruitlessly though laboriously occupying Folly and Seabrook Islands, and such
other troops as can be spared from the remaining posts of this department, to penetrate
into Georgia, produce a practical dissolution
of the slave system there, destroy all railroad
communication along the eastern portion of
the State, and lay waste all stores which
can possibly be used for the sustenance of
the rebellion.

My troops are in splendid health and discipline, and, in my judgment, are more
thoroughly in sympathy with the policy of
the Government than any other equal body
of men in the service of the United States
to-day. With the exception of one brigadier-
general and one colonel commanding a
brigade, there is not an officer of any con-
sequence in the command who is not heart
and soul in favor of prosecuting this war by
every and any means likely to ensure success.

Only once liberate me from enforced waiting on the action of those who, I fear, are not likely to do anything, and I promise you that I will give full employment to twice or thrice my number of the enemy ; and that while ROSECRANS threatens BRAGG in front, I will interrupt his communications, threaten his rear, and spread a panic through the country.

In this connection, I would ask, if possible, for a regiment of cavalry, and that the brigade sent by me to the relief of Major-General FOSTER may be ordered back from North Carolina. If no cavalry can be spared, then that five hundred horses and a thousand saddles and equipments may be sent to me immediately. Also, that the pikes drawn for my chief of ordnance may be supplied immediately ; these weapons being the simplest and most effective than can be placed in the hands of the slaves who are liberated in our march into the interior.

In conclusion, I would again call attention to my request to be endowed with the same powers entrusted to Adjutant-General THOMAS, for raising colored regiments and giving commissions to their officers. I think this of the utmost importance, as each commission promptly given to a deserving non-commissioned officer or private, has the effect of conciliating the sentiment of the regiment from which the appointee is taken ; and it is of the utmost importance that the experiment of colored soldiers should have the hearty acquiescence of the troops with whom they serve.

I deem this matter of so much importance, and am so weary of inactivity, that I send this letter by special steamer to Fortress Monroe, and have instructed the captain of the vessel to wait for your reply.

I have the honor to be, sir,

Very respectfully,

Your obedient servant,

(Signed) D. HUNTER,

Major-General Commanding.

His Excellency A. LINCOLN,

President of the United States.

I send this letter by Captain ARTHUR M. KINZIE, one of my aides-de-camp, who will await your answer, and return immediately by the steamer which bears this to Fortress Monroe.

(Signed)   D. HUNTER,

Major-General.

This letter was published in the Report of the Hon. Secretary of the navy on "Armored Vessels," made by order of Congress, in 1864, pages 110, 111, and 112.

I was "temporarily" relieved from the command of the Department of the South, in order to give another officer an opportunity to try his plans for the reduction of Fort Sumter and the City of Charleston. In reference to this suspension of my command, I addressed to Mr. LINCOLN the following note, dated June 25, 1863:

PRINCETON, NEW JERSEY, June 25, 1863.

To His EXCELLENCY A. LINCOLN,

President of the United States:

SIR: You cannot fail to be aware that my removal from the command of the Department of the South has been all but universally regarded as a censure on my conduct, while in that command,

Satisfied and well knowing that I acted throughout in strict obedience to orders, and that my record when published will prove an ample vindication of my course, I now respectfully request of you liberty to make such publication of official documents and records as may be necessary to set me right in the eyes of my friends, and in the justice of history. The time has now passed when any injurious effect to the public service could possibly arise from such publication.

Knowing how greatly your time is occupied, I shall regard your silence in reply to this note as giving me the liberty I ask, and will act accordingly. Should you deem such publications as I propose unadvisable, will you be kind enough to notify me of your opinion without delay?

I have the honor to be, sir,

Very respectfully,

Your most obedient servant,

DAVID HUNTER,

Major-General.

To this letter I received a kind but not alto-gether satisfactory reply, which is as follows :

EXECUTIVE MANSION, WASHINGTON,
June 30, 1863.

MY DEAR GENERAL : I have just received your letter of the 25th of June.

I assure you, and you may feel authorized in stating, that the recent change of command-ers in the Department of the South was made for no reasons which convey any imputation upon your known energy, efficiency, and pa-triotism ; but for causes which seemed suffi-cient while they were in no degree incompat-ible with the respect and esteem in which I have always held you as a man and an officer.

I cannot, by giving my consent to a pub-lication of whose details I know nothing, as-sume the responsibility of whatever you may write. In this matter, your own sense of mili-tary propriety must be your guide, and the regulations of the service your rule of conduct.

I am, very truly,

Your friend,

A. LINCOLN.

Major-Gen. HUNTER.

The latter paragraph of this letter refers to my earnest request to be relieved from the operation of the Army Regulation forbidding commanding generals making any publications with regard to military affairs. I made this request because I knew that serious misapprehensions prevailed in reference to my Department, which no one was able to correct but myself.

Mr. LINCOLN informed me that the temporary suspension of my command, above alluded to, was due in a great measure to the influence of the Hon. HORACE GREELEY. The knowledge of that fact induced me to address the following letter to Mr. GREELEY :

PORT ROYAL, SOUTH CAROLINA,
June 12, 1863.

H. GREELEY. *Esq.. New York:*

SIR : Since you have undertaken the attack on Charleston, I sincerly hope you will be more successful than in your first advance on Richmond, in which you wasted much ink, and other men shed some blood. It is clear from your paper that you knew nothing of the orders which bound me to a particular course of action, which orders I strictly followed, and for obeying which I am censured. Worse than any wound our enemies can inflict, are the stabs in the dark of pretended friends. The country must be informed that you have charge of this second attack on Charleston, so that on you may rest the praise or censure.

Very respectfully,

Your most ob. servant,

D. HUNTER.

It may not be out of place to state that Fort Sumter remained unreduced until the end of the war, and was then stronger than at the beginning.

PROPOSED EXPEDITIONS THROUGH THE GULF STATES.

It will be seen by my letter of the 22d of May, 1863, to the President, previously given, that I urged him in the strongest terms to be liberated from the order to " co-operate with the navy in an attack on Charleston," well know-

ing that Admiral Du Pont had declared he
would not fire another gun, and to be permitted to make an expedition into the heart
of Georgia, our landing and marching being
made through counties in which, as shown by
the census, the slave population is seventy-five
per cent. of the inhabitants.

And, in my letter to the Hon. Secretary of
War of the 31st of August, 1863, I begged to
be permitted to land a force at Brunswick,
Georgia, and march through Georgia, Alabama, and Mississippi, arming all the negroes
as I advanced, and striking for New Orleans.

And again, in my letter to Mr. Stanton,
from Louisville, Ky., I say :

" There are now crowded into the States of
Alabama and Georgia near two millions of
negroes, furnishing four hundred thousand
fighting men, all ready, willing, and anxious to
be drafted, and making much better soldiers
than most of the men who require six and
seven hundred dollars to induce them to '*vol-
unteer.*' Twenty, fifteen, or even ten thousand
men, marched rapidly into these State, without baggage, without artillery, subsisting on

the country, carrying arms and ammunition for the negroes, and officers enough for one hundred thousand men, could go, without serious opposition, directly from Vicksburg to Charleston. I think you will find that this small force can now well be spared, and I am confident it could march from the Mississippi to the Atlantic without serious opposition. A general rebellion among those crowded negroes would certainly produce great demoralization throughout the rebel army. The corn crop is very abundant, and if we can get nothing else we can live on the corn. We certainly should be able to do whatever the rebels can. The negroes would know every path, as they make most of their visits in the night, and we should thus be able to march just as well at night as in the day.

" I beg you will telegraph me to this place authority to take charge of an expedition of this kind.

" I have the honor to be, very respectfully,

"DAVID HUNTER,

Major-General."

Mr. STANTON informed me that both Mr. LINCOLN and himself approved this plan, but that a sufficient number of men could not at that time be spared for the attempt.

In the fall of 1803, I was ordered by the Hon. Secretary of War to inspect all the troops in the Valley of the Mississippi, under command of General GRANT. I was with Gen. GRANT at the battle of Mission Ridge, on the 23d, 24th, and 25th November, 1803. My inspection duties continued until April, 1864. I was then ordered to visit General BANKS, at that time in command at Alexandria, La., on the Red River.

CAMPAIGN IN THE VALLEY OF VIRGINIA.

On my return from the Red River, I was ordered to the command of the Department of West Virginia, May 19, 1864. For a complete account of my operations in this department, I beg to refer to the report of my Chief of Staff, General D. H. STROTHER —annexed to this report.

The importance of our attack on Lynchburg was fully appreciated by the enemy.

General STROTHER, a native Virginian, spent the first year after the war in Richmond. His official position, as Secretary of State and Adjutant-General of Virginia, brought him into contact with many of the ex-rebel officers, who all spoke in strong terms of the great injury our raid inflicted on the Confederacy.

Mr. JEFFERSON DAVIS also, in his speech to the people of Georgia, at Macon, after the fall of Atlanta, said: "An audacious movement of the enemy up to the very walls of Lynchburg had rendered it necessary that the Government should send a formidable body of troops to cover that vital point, which had otherwise been intended for the relief of Atlanta."

The following despatch from General GRANT to the Assistant Secretary of War relates to the same subject:

HEADQUARTERS, ARMIES OF THE UNITED STATES,
CITY POINT, VA., July 15, 1864.

C. A. DANA, *Acting Secretary of War:*

I am sorry to see such a disposition to condemn a brave old soldier, as General HUNTER is known to be, without a hearing. He is known to have advanced into the enemy's country, towards their main army, inflicted a much greater damage upon them, than they have inflicted upon us, with double his force, and moving directly away from our main army. HUNTER acted, too, in a country where he had no friends, whilst the enemy have only operated in territory, where, to say the least, many of the inhabitants are their friends.

If General HUNTER has made war on the newspapers in West Virginia, probably he has done right.

I fail to see yet that General HUNTER has not acted with great promptness and great success. Even the enemy give him great credit for courage, and congratulate themselves that he will give them a chance of getting even with him.

U. S. GRANT,

Lieut.-General.

I was, at my own request, relieved from the command of the Department of West Virginia, August 8, 1864.

COURTS-MARTIAL AND COMMISSIONS.

As already stated, I acted as President of
the Court-Martial, convened 23d September,
1862, for the trial of General FITZJOHN
PORTER. On the 1st of February, 1865, I
was President of the Court-Martial which
met at Paducah, Ky., for the trial of Brigadier-General E. A. PAINE, of Illinois ; Colonel
WM. McK. DUNN being the Judge-Advocate of the Court.

I was also President of the Court of Enquiry, of which General EDMUND SCHRIVER,
Inspector-General, was Recorder, which met
at Nashville, Tenn., and Louisville, Ky., in
the fall of 1863, to enquire into the conduct
of Generals McCOOK, CRITTENDEN, and NEG-
LEY, at the battle of Chickamauga, September 19 and 20, 1863.

In April, 1865, I was detailed as one of the
general officers to accompany the remains of
President LINCOLN to Springfield, Illinois, but
was recalled by a telegram from the Hon.
Secretary of War, to preside at the Military
Commission convened for the trial of the
assassins of the President, which met in this

city on the 9th of May, 1865. Of that Commission, Gen. JOSEPH HOLT, Judge-Advocate General, was the Judge-Advocate, assisted by the Hon. JOHN A. BINGHAM, of Ohio.

I was on duty during the fall of 1866 as President of the Special Claims Commission, and as President of the Board for the examination of officers promoted to the cavalry.

BREVET RANK.

I was brevetted a Brigadier-General in the United States Army on the 13th of March, 1865, for gallant and meritorious services at the battle of Piedmont, and during the campaign in the Valley of Virginia ; and a Major-General in the United States Army, March 13, 1865, for gallant and meritorious services during the Rebellion.